OLDER CAN BE BOLDER:

101 answers to your questions about aging

By

Erdman B. Palmore, Ph.D.

Professor Emeritus of Medical Sociology
Duke University Center for the Study of Aging

I dedicate this book to my children and

grandchildren

who inspire me to grow bolder.

PREFACE

Some people grow timid as they age because they are afraid of aging. They haven't heard the good news about aging: you can grow *bolder* as you grow *older*. Many people are afraid to ask the questions answered in this book because they think only about the problems of aging and not the benefits of aging. The answers in this book recognize the problems, but also the many advantages of aging, such as:

* You keep on living! Most important, because the alternative to aging is dying.

* You don't have to work anymore if you don't want to.

* You can work part time if you want to.

* You can do more volunteer work if you want to.

* You don't have to dress up everyday to go to the office or business.

* You can start a new career without worrying about whether you can live on the income.

* You can start that hobby you never got started before retirement.

* You don't need an alarm clock (usually).

* You can stay up as late as you want and sleep as late as you want.

* You can have as many naps as you want.

* You can travel whenever you want.

* You have more time for family and friends.

* You usually have grandchildren to enjoy.

* You become the patriarch or matriarch of your family.

* You don't have to take care of the kids, unless you want to.

* You're free from most family responsibilities.

* You don't have to worry about becoming pregnant.

* Your income from Social Security is inflation proof.

* You have a guaranteed annual income from the government (SSI).

* You have national health insurance (Medicare).

* You can get a lot of senior discounts.

* You can order senior portions in restaurants to save money and stay thin.

* You can get priority seating on buses, subway cars, etc.

* You can be the first to leave a party and nobody questions it.

* You will become less likely to be a victim of crime.

* You will be less likely to have an accident in your home.

* You will be less likely to have an accident on the highway.

* You will be less likely to have an accident on the job.

* You will be less likely to have a mental illness.

* You will have less acute illnesses.

* You will be less likely to become alcoholic.

* You will be less likely to become addicted to drugs.

* You can improve your physical function as you grow older.

* You are likely to learn more about civic affairs and vote more often.

* You will have more years of experience.

* You can get wiser from you experience.

* You will have greater life satisfaction.

* You can gather material for memoirs, photo albums, and scrap books.

* You probably will grow more tolerant.

* Your relationships usually improve.

* You can become less inhibited.

* You can prove it's never too late to learn.

* Your gray hairs usually get respect.

* You can brag about your age.

* You become a survivor.

    This book will not only answer your questions about aging, but it can

help you look forward to the advantages of aging and to become proud of your age! Each birthday can become a cause for celebration rather than

something to be ashamed of. Here's a toast "To Life!"

Does strength decline?

Does lung capacity decline?

Do all five senses diminish?

Why do eyes tend to water more with old age?

Are older workers less productive?

Can most old people do normal activities without help?

Why do older men urinate so often?

Can old people still enjoy sex?

Is there a male menopause?

CHAPTER THREE: MENTAL HEALTH

Why do we forget the things we want to remember and remember the things we want to forget?

Does aging impair your memory?

How can you preserve your memory?

Are there memory aids that really work?

What causes Alzheimer's disease?

Can Alzheimer's disease be prevented?

Can Alzheimer's disease be cured?

What causes Parkinson's disease?

Can Vitamin C increase longevity?

Can eating less increase longevity?

Can yogurt increase longevity?

Are there longevity zones?

Why do women live longer than men?

Why are there more widows than widowers?

Why do Whites live longer than Blacks?

Is longevity increasing?

CHAPTER FIVE: AGEISM

What is ageism?

What are the most frequent forms of ageism?

Is ageism as bad as racism or sexism?

Is ageism declining?

Are old people more conservative?

Are old people set in their ways?

Will there be a war between the generations?

How do old people contribute to our economy?

Can old people understand young people?

Are jokes about old people ageism?

Are attempts to look younger a kind of ageism?

Is "You don't look that old" a kind of ageism?

What causes ageism?

What are the effects of ageism?

Are old people crime victims more often than young people?

Why are old people more afraid of crime?

Are there fewer criminals among old people?

Do doctors discriminate against old people?

Are old people often isolated and lonely?

Are old people often cranky or angry?

Is there more poverty among old people?

Do most old people have fixed incomes?

Is there a Senior Voting Bloc?

Are there more older people in public office than younger?

How can we reduce ageism?

CHAPTER SIX: BENEFITS

Are old people bankrupting the government?

Are old people pushing up the cost of medical care?

Should health care be rationed by age?

Are organ transplants worthwhile in old age?

Do most old people end up in institutions?

Are most caregivers young people?

Do old people get more than their share of the national income?

When do you become entitled to Social Security?

When do you become entitled to Supplemental Security Income?

When do you become entitled to Medicare?

Does Medicare cover most medical expenses?

When do you become entitled to Medicaid?

What tax breaks can elders get?

When can you join AARP?

When can you get senior discounts?

How many benefits are there to aging?

CHAPTER ONE: APPEARANCE

What is aging?

Age is just a number. -Anonymous

Age is strictly a case of mind over matter – if you don't mind it don't matter.

-Anonymous

These two answers are valid from the standpoint of chronological aging. Strictly speaking, aging is simply the passage of time. However, most people associate aging with the changes in appearance that we will discuss in this chapter. Friedrich Schiller wrote, "Appearance rules the world." We think this is a shallow view of aging, but since it is a common view we will begin with appearances in aging.

Other chapters will answer questions about other aspects of aging: changes in physical and mental health, as well as longevity, ageism, and entitlements. But remember: "age is just a number" and aging doesn't really cause anything.

Why do men get bald?

I'm not getting bald—I just have a long face.-Anonymous

This kind of denial reflects the fear of appearing to be "old." Actually, balding (alopecia) may be caused by illness, stress, x-rays, chemotherapy, and genetics, but the most common cause of normal balding is a male hormone called, dihydrotestosterone (DHA). This form of testosterone is caused by an enzyme created mainly in the prostate (5-alpha reductase). That is why eunuchs castrated before puberty don't become bald: they do not have much testosterone. So if you are obsessed with keeping your hair, you might try castration (although that is rather permanent).

As normal men get older, their DHA tends to increase (relative to their estrogen), and this causes the balding. Thus, balding in men is a sign of their masculinity (more testosterone)! The male pattern of balding starts at the front hairline and spreads backward. Balding can happen to women also, although female pattern balding tends to be diffuse over the top of the scalp while retaining the frontal hairline.

Why do older women grow beards?

If you grow a beard, you don't have to shave. -Anonymous

This is the reverse problem of balding, but stems from a similar process. After menopause, the ratio of male hormones (androgen) to female hormones (estrogens) tends to increase in women. This can increase facial hair, but the amount of facial hair is largely hereditary. However, some medical conditions may also cause facial hair growth among women. So if you are an older woman growing a moustache or beard, it would be wise to check with your doctor.

Why does hair turn grey?

"I've reached the metallic age: I've got silver in my hair, gold in my teeth and lead in my rear."-Anonymous

Actually, there is no such thing as a "grey hair". Hairs are either a dark color or white. The illusion of grey hair is produced by the mixture of white to dark hairs in which the white hairs predominate. The increase of white hairs is caused by a reduction in melanin produced by the melanocytes in the hair bulb. This is an irreversible process, so unless we want to deny our age, we might as well develop the attitude that "grey is beautiful"!

Why do we grow wrinkles?

These aren't wrinkles; they are "laugh lines". -Anonymous

Wrinkles are honorable insignia of long service in this warfare. –Bob Phillips

The most striking characteristic of older skin is the flattening of the dermo-epidermal junction, which results in wrinkles. You can actually guess a person's age by the "pinch test". Put your hand down on a flat surface and gently pinch up the skin on the back of your hand, and count how long it takes to return to normal when you let it go. The skin on a young person's hand will snap back down instantly; skin on middle-aged person will take two or three second to go down; skin on an older person may take five or more seconds.

Genetics, nutrition, disease, and exposure to sunlight may all play a role in causing wrinkles; but the greatest of these is sunlight (or its equivalent, sun tanning bulbs). So the best way to avoid wrinkles is to pick parents with few wrinkles, eat healthy stuff, and stay out of the sun.

Or you can decide that wrinkles make you look distinguished and not worry about it!

Why do wrinkles get worse after a long bath?

"Are you getting old or have you been taking long baths?"-Anonymous

People of all ages may get the "pruney look", especially on their hands and feet, after soaking in a tub. This is caused by the outer layer of skin (epidermis) absorbing some of the water and expanding, while the layer below (dermis) does not expand, so the epidermis buckles in some areas. This is especially noticeable on the hands and feet because the skin is thicker in these areas. If this bothers you, just take quick showers instead of soaking baths. Personally, I think a relaxing long hot bath is worth a few wrinkles!

Can wrinkles be removed?

She had her face lifted so many times, her face is out of focus. -Anonymous

Most of the over-the-counter "wrinkle removers" and "skin rejuvenators" have no scientific evidence to support their claims. Their effectiveness is only supported by testimonials and anecdotes – and it's easy to pay people to testify that any nostrum is "marvelously" effective.

Tretinoin (Retin-A) is the only topical medication that has been proven to temporarily reduce wrinkles. However, tretinoin increases sensitivity to sunlight, so you need to avoid sunlight or use protective clothing when using it. Also there are side effects such as peeling, dry skin, burning, itching, and redness. All these problems raise the question as to whether it is worthwhile, all things considered.

But, yes, wrinkles can be temporarily removed in several ways: Botox, cosmetic surgery, chemical peels, and laser resurfacing. The main problem with all these methods is they are dangerous. Botox treatments are especially dangerous because they involve injections of the Botulinum toxin under the skin in the area of wrinkles, which paralyses the muscles and gives the appearance of smoother skin. (A side effect is a mask-like appearance because of the paralyzed facial muscles.) However, this effect lasts for only a few weeks or months at most, after which the wrinkles reappear. Furthermore, there have been over 180 reports of adverse side effects, including 16 deaths.

Face lifts or other types of plastic surgery are also dangerous because they are invasive surgery. This means that there are the unavoidable dangers of infection, side effects of anesthesia, etc. of any invasive surgery. Most dangers can be avoided by a skilled surgeon and proper follow-up, but the scars that result from it may be difficult to hide. Furthermore, you will probably need to repeat the face lift in a few years, if you want to prevent the return of your wrinkles.

Chemical peels and laser resurfacing involve destroying the outer surface of the skin and waiting for it to grow back in, which involves considerable pain and redness.

Since all these procedures have only temporary effects, the short answer is, wrinkles cannot be removed permanently.

Why do elders tend to get bags under their eyes?

"Don't call her a 'bag lady' just because she has bags under her eyes!"- *Anonymous*

Actually, bags under the eyes or dark rings can occur at any age and are caused by lack of restful sleep, poor nutrition, or illness. The skin around the eyes is the thinnest skin on the body, and therefore the dark, venous blood can show through making the appearance of bags or dark rings. So this can be prevented by good sleep, nutrition, and health – or you can just wear dark glasses all the time.

What are actinic keratoses?

"Lots of sunshine is good for you." – Mother

This is what my Mother told me and encouraged me to stay in the sun for hours (resulting in a lot of sunburn). This belief is rapidly being replaced by warnings of the dangers of over-exposure to sunlight. One of the primary dangers is actinic keratoses, or "sunspots", which are actually lesions on the skin caused by exposure to ultra-violet rays. These lesions tend to harden and peel and then harden again. They are considered pre-cancerous because they may develop into skin cancers. They can be removed in various ways, but prevention by using sun blockers and covering up is "worth a pound of cure."

However, it is true that a "moderate" amount of sunshine may be beneficial by creating Vitamin D in the skin. The danger for light-skinned people (blonds & red-heads) is that any exposure over a half-hour or so may be dangerous. Furthermore, if you already have actinic keratosis, even a few minutes exposure to the sun is likely to make them worse. It is probably safer to get your Vitamin D from enriched milk and/or pills.

What are "age spots?"

These spots, also known as sunspots or lentigines, are brown spots which also occur where the skin has been exposed to the sun for many years. They are caused by an increase in the number of pigment-producing cells and by thinning of the skin with age, which makes the spots more obvious. However, they are not harmful and do not lead to skin cancer – so don't worry about them.

Do ears and noses grow with age?

Do your ears hang low; do they wobble to and fro? Can you tie 'em in a knot; can you tie 'em in a bow?-Anonymous song

We used to sing this song when we were kids, and it may come from an exaggerated fear of aging because ears do continue to grow with age. Your nose can also continue to grow. Both of these effects are caused by the continued growth of cartilage in these appendages.

Why do old people have longer teeth?

"Grandma, why are your teeth so long?" -Goldilocks

A similar process is the lengthening of teeth with age, especially when the opposing tooth has been lost. Cementum is deposited continuously throughout life at the root apex and the interradicular surfaces as the tooth undergoes slow growth. However, teeth may appear to be longer than they actually are, because shrinkage of the gums exposes more of the tooth to view.

Why do you shrink as you get older?

It's better to have loved a short man than never to have loved a'tall. - Anonymous

Extra tall people may look forward to shrinking down to a more normal height, while short people can do some things to reduce this shrinkage. It can be caused by several processes. Reduced calcium absorption can make the bone segments shrink, so extra calcium and Vitamin D in your diet may help prevent this. Obesity or poor nutrition can cause the cartilage discs between the bones to shrink. The loss of muscle in your back and poor posture may make you slump down, so exercises for the back and better posture may reduce this cause.

Why do old people tend to get fat?

I'm on a "see food diet:" I see food and eat it. -Anonymous

A big man has no time really to do anything but sit and be big. –F. Scott Fitzgerald.

There are two major causes of getting fat in old age. First, metabolism tends to slow down, so calories are not burned up as rapidly as by younger people. Therefore, more calories tend to be converted into fat and it is more difficult to burn the fat calories when trying to reduce. The way to compensate for this, obviously, is to eat less calories (although this is "easier said than done").

Second, most people tend to become less active with age, just when they should become more active because of their slowing metabolism. The iron law of body weight applies at all ages: "Body weight equals calories in, minus calories out." Remember: "The rocking chair can be deadly in old age".

CHAPTER TWO: PHYSICAL FUNCTION

Does your body wear out?

I got this dress for my 18th birthday.

It certainly wore well, didn't it?-Anonymous

Dresses and other inanimate things can wear out, but most parts of our body do not literally "wear out." Teeth are the only organs that "wear out," in the dictionary sense of "to make useless by long or hard usage." Most of the rest of our body normally can repair itself. Of course, disease and trauma can interfere with this ability to self-repair – at any age. Also physical functions can decline from atrophy at any age. The old adage, "Use it or lose it," is especially relevant for old age.

Does strength decline?

My strength is as the strength of ten, because my heart is pure. -
Tennyson

So, according to Tennyson, if elders just keep their heart pure, their strength should not decline. Unfortunately,
muscular strength and endurance does tend to decline with age, but much of this decline can be counteracted by increased exercise, better nutrition, and a

healthy life-style. In fact, strength can even be increased by most people because they are so far below their maximum functional abilities.

I am trying to prove that you can improve strength and endurance with age by increasing my training each year so that I can ride my age (81) in miles on my bicycle and do my age in push-ups, sit-ups, and knee bends.

Does lung capacity decline?

TB or not TB; that is the congestion. –Take off from Hamlet's soliloquy.

Even though you have not had TB, some aspects of lung capacity do tend to decline and some don't. While vital lung capacity (as measured by the volume of air that can be expelled in one breath) tends to decline, residual volume tends to increase, so that total lung capacity tends to remain high even in old age. Also cardio-vascular exercise, especially breathing exercise, can counteract the loss of vital lung capacity.

Do all five senses diminish?

See no evil, hear no evil, speak no evil. –Japanese proverb

Older people could add: taste no evil, smell no evil, and touch no evil, because all five senses do tend to weaken in old age. Taste sensitivity tends to gradually diminish in normal aging primarily because of changes in the taste cell membranes, as well as the loss of some taste buds. However, a major cause is medication that can reduce taste sensitivity. Studies have implicated over 250 drugs that alter taste sensations.

Losses in odor perception result primarily from anatomic and physiological changes in the nose, olfactory bulbs, and certain brain structures. However, loss of both taste and odor sensitivity may be caused by disease, smoking, viruses, head trauma, surgery, and pollution in the environment.

Touch sensitivity also tends to diminish after age 45, but the good news is that so does sensitivity to pain. The ability to detect vibration normally declines only in the lower extremities.

Vision is the major way most of us perceive our environment and it tends to decline with age for several reasons: changes in the lens, the pupil, and light adaptation. However, the good news is that at age 80, 70 percent of drivers are still qualified for unrestricted driving, and another 15 percent are qualified to drive in the daytime only. Fortunately, eye glasses and improved lighting can correct most age-related vision problems.

Hearing is the second major sense and as people grow older they tend to have more difficulty hearing high-pitched sounds and low intensity sounds. However, hearing aids are usually able to overcome at least some of this hearing loss. Here again, "Prevention is the best cure." Avoid abusing your ears with prolonged deafening noises such as rock concerts, high fidelity speakers turned up to their maxim, chain saws, and industrial noise (without ear plugs).

Why do eyes tend to water more with old age?

"I'm not crying. These are tears of joy!" -Anonymous

Watery eyes are caused by a combination of eye lids loosening so that some of the normal eye fluids may leak out, and less efficient fluid absorption by the tissues next to the nose which are supposed to pump the fluid out of the eyes. This is no cause for alarm and the only problem may be that your handkerchief gets damp from wiping up the tears.

Are older workers less productive?

Older worker to younger worker: "You're not supposed to smoke while working."

Younger worker: "Who says I'm working?"-Anonymous

The majority of older workers can be as productive as younger workers. Despite declines in perception and reaction speed among the general aged population, studies of employed older workers under actual working conditions generally show that they perform as well as, if not better than, younger workers. When speed and accuracy of movement are important to the job, some studies do show declines with age. However, intellectual ability, on which much of work performance depends, does not decline substantially until the 80s in most individuals. Also consistency of output tends to increase with age, and older workers have less job turnover, fewer accidents, and less absenteeism than others.

Can most old people do normal activities without help?

Some of our modern grandmothers are so young and spry they help Boy Scouts across the street. -Anonymous

More than 85% of people over 65 are able to do their basic activities of daily living without help, such as eating, bathing, and dressing. Another 10% need help and 5% are in long-term care institutions such as nursing homes.

Why do older men have to urinate so often?

Two problems: some men have trouble starting and others have trouble stopping. -Anonymous

The usual cause of frequent urination in older men is Benign Prostatic Hypertrophy (BPH), or enlargement of the prostate gland. This enlargement constricts the urethra so that the bladder is not completely emptied when urinating. Thus, the bladder fills up again rapidly and causes the frequent urge to urinate. Another cause is detrusor instability, which is overactivity of the bladder muscle.

Can old people still enjoy sex?

I'm not as good as I once was, but I am still good once as I was. -

Anonymous

Over the hill and off the pill. -Anonymous

The majority of persons past age 65 continue to have both interest in and capacity for sexual intercourse and/or masturbation. Most older persons report that sex after age 65 is as satisfying or more satisfying than when they were younger. This is because they no longer fear pregnancy, have more time for leisurely love-making, are not worried about interruptions from children, are less worried about their career, have learned how to be better lovers, etc. Frequency of sexual intercourse is mainly controlled by the availability of a partner; but many of those without partners continue to have orgasms through masturbation. Furthermore, cuddling and caressing can continue to be delightful, with or without intercourse.

Is there a male menopause?

Be ready when the moment is right. –Commercial for Cialis

This is a controversial question. Some believe that there is such a thing called the Aging Male Syndrome (AMS) caused by the decrease in testosterone that is normal in older men. The symptoms include erectile dysfunction (ED), lethargy, depression, and decrease in lean muscle. Many men receive treatment with testosterone and report improvement in symptoms. The danger of this may be an increased risk of prostate cancer and atherosclerosis. Many gerontologists believe that AMS is more likely to be the result of non-hormonal aging processes. These days ED is usually treated with Viagra, Cialis, or other such drugs. Apparently most men can continue to enjoy orgasms and produce ejaculations well into their 80's or beyond. Furthermore, most men do not "run out of sperm." Many older men have been able to maintain a normal sperm count.

CHAPTER THREE. MENTAL HEALTH

Why do we forget the things we want to remember and remember the things we want to forget?

I got some pills to improve my memory, but I keep forgetting to take them. - Anonymous

The main reasons we forget things we want to remember are lack of attention and/or insufficient processing. In order for something to be remembered, we must first pay close attention to it so we can clearly perceive it. We need to avoid distractions and competing thoughts or images. Then we need to process it to move it into the long-term memory banks. This processing can be by repeating it to ourselves, or rehearsing it, or building up some kind of visual or temporal association, or attaching some kind of label or clue for future recall. The more ways we process it and the more time we spend processing it, the better we will remember it.

The main reason we remember things we want to forget is the reverse of why we forget: we pay too much attention to it and process it over and over. It does no good to say to yourself, "Forget XYZ! Don't think about XYZ!" The mental command, "Forget XYZ!" actually refreshes XYZ in your memory. A better strategy is to concentrate on something else that you *do* want to remember – preferably something pleasant.

Does aging impair your memory?

"My memory is not getting better, but my "forgettory" is getting stronger."
–My Father

Up until about 10 years ago, brain researchers equated age-related memory loss with brain cell death. But thanks to recent neural imaging techniques, they discovered that aging itself does not cause a significant loss of neurons in the *hippocampus,* a part of the brain involved in storing and retrieving memories. Furthermore, the good news is that new neurons may even be added to the hippocampus in adulthood – which destroys the old belief adults can't grow new brain cells.

Now it appears that, if there is some memory loss with aging, it is probably caused by a reduction in the chemicals that facilitate communication and coordination between different parts of the brain. The bottom line is that memory loss is not an inevitable withering away of neurons; and that there are things you can do to preserve and boost your memories.

How can you preserve your memory?

"What's the name of that course you're taking to improve your memory?"

"I can't remember." -Anonymous

There are a bunch of things you can do to preserve and boost your memory:

* Exercise your brain. Although the brain is not a muscle, it responds to exercise like a muscle: if you exercise it, it tends to maintain its strength; if you don't use it much, it tends to wither; memories tend to atrophy. Apparently any kind of challenge to your mind can work as brain exercise: solving puzzles; playing games; memorizing poems and songs; learning a new language; taking or teaching a course; writing; using a computer; reading something mentally challenging; playing a musical instrument; dancing; doing a routine task in a novel way (like using your left hand if you're right handed, and vice versa).

* Process information with several senses: visual, auditory, and touch.

* Avoid excessive stress. A little stress may be good to challenge your brain, but too much stress that makes you anxious or depressed is not good.

* Get plenty of sleep. Most old people need as much or more sleep as younger people. Short naps during the day are also beneficial.

* Stay involved with people. People with larger social networks tend to maintain their mental functions better than isolated people, because social people are more likely to engage in the physical and mental activities which boost brain function.

* Do volunteer work. Volunteer work tends to challenge brains with new activities, exercise, and socializing. It also makes you feel useful and valued, which helps prevent depression.

* Take care of your body. Your brain is part of your body, so keeping your body healthy through regular exercise, good diet, hygiene, and medical care is essential for brain health.

* Eat a brain-healthy diet: lots of fruits and vegetables, whole grains, fish like salmon, tuna, and sardines (rich in omega-3 fatty acids).

Are there memory aids that really work?

Memory aids work if you can just remember them. -Anonymous

Here is a list of tried and true memory aids that really work (and are easy to remember).

*Write it down. The act of writing itself helps to process the memory as well as serving as a reminder if it is written on your calendar or posted in a prominent place.

* Create a visual image. This helps process the memory into another area of the memory banks.

* Associate it with something you already know, connect the memory with another one, such as another similar name or word or image.

* Memorize small chunks at a time. Think of a phone number as three chunks (area code, the exchange, and the individual number), not one long number.

* Be consistent about where you put things. Designate only one or two places that you put down your glasses or keys or wallet or hearing aid. Do not put your wallet away until you have put your credit card back in it.

* Look for visual clues. To remember where you parked, look for specific landmarks, or write down the number of the space.

* Set a timer to remind you to take care of something, like turn off a burner or wake up from a nap.

What causes Alzheimer's disease?

One good thing about Alzheimer's disease: you keep meeting new friends. - Anonymous

We are not yet sure what causes Alzheimer's Disease (AD); but there is evidence to support several theories:

* Environmental toxins such as aluminum, lead, and mercury

* Viral infections

* Bacterial infections

* Prions (proteinaceous infectious particles)

* Autoimmunity

* Genetics: the presence of apolipoprotein E-4 (Apo E-4), a gene found on chromosome 19, markedly increases the risk of AD. Also having a parent with AD doubles the risk of AD

* Head injuries

* Hypertension

* High blood levels of homocysteine, an amino acid

* High cholesterol levels

Can Alzheimer's Disease be prevented?

Since you can't prevent Alzheimer's, you might as well forget about it. -

Anonymous

That saying is not good advice. Although it is true that there is no vaccine to prevent AD (yet) and no way to completely prevent AD, there are many things that can delay or reduce the risk of AD. The tips (above) on how to preserve your memory also can reduce the risk of AD. In addition, the following may also help ward off AD:

*Get treatment for anxiety or depression.

*Eat a healthy low-fat diet that includes weekly servings of fish high in amega-3 fatty acids.

* Drink alcohol moderately (one or two ounces of alcohol, four ounces of wine, daily).

* Take a multivitamin/mineral tablet without iron.

* Try stress management techniques such as yoga or transcendental meditation.

* Reduce high blood pressure.

* Reduce high cholesterol levels.

Can Alzheimer's Disease be cured?

The only cure for AD is death. -Anonymous

This grim "joke" reflects the grim fact that despite all the research and all the claims for "cures", there is not yet any proven cure for AD. However, just because AD is incurable does not mean that it is *untreatable*. There are several medications that have been proven to slow and even stop

(temporarily) the progression of AD:

* Aricept (donepezil) – May help at all stages of AD.

* Exelon (rivastigmine) – May help in mild to moderate stages.

* Razadyne (galantamine) – May help in mild to moderate stages.

* Namenda (memantine) – May help in moderate to severe stages.

There are also several other medications that are currently in clinical trials

and hold promise for future treatment. However, Vitamin E, which was

thought to slow the progression of AD in mild cases, has now been shown to

be ineffective.

What causes Parkinson's Disease?

Which is worse: Alzheimer's or Parkinson's Disease?-Anonymous

This is a highly debatable question, because each disease has its advantages

or disadvantages compared to the other. AD inevitably involves dementia

while Parkinson patients may escape this, at least for many years. On the

other hand, Parkinson patients are usually faced with tremors, rigidity,

eventual loss of mobility and ability to respond at all.

As for the causes of Parkinson's, there are three main groups: postencephalitic, arteriroscleriotic, and idiopathic. Postencephalitic Parkinson's is caused by a history of encephalitis lethargica. Arteriroscleriotic Parkinson's is caused by multiinfarcts in the brain. About 85% of Parkinson patients have idiopathic causes – which simply means the causes are unknown.

Can Parkinson's Disease be cured?

The answer to this question is similar to the answer for Alzheimer's – not at present. However there are several treatments that can relieve the symptoms – at least temporarily:

* Levodopa (L-dopa) can reduce the severity of the motor disorder and improve the quality of life in the majority of patients for a while.

* Anticholinergic drugs which are less frequently employed today because of bad side-effects such as memory impairment.

* Dopamine agonists which stimulate the dopaminergic cells.

* Neurosurgery which may include destruction of specific areas of the basal ganglia or implantation of microstimulators.

Are old people more depressed?

The older we get, the fewer things seem worth waiting in line for. -

Anonymous

Depression is among the most common complaints of older adults.

However, the good news is that major depressive disorders (not counting

those due to bereavement) is less than half as prevalent among persons over

65 as in the general population. It appears that most older adults have

learned how to "look on the bright side" and not let the vicissitudes of aging

make them clinically depressed. They have learned how to expect and

accept the various problems of aging as part of living.

However, it is true that because depression is easily confused with other

conditions, such as dementia and hypochondriasis, depressed older adults are

often undiagnosed.

Can depression be cured?

"Leave your worries on the doorstep. Life can be so sweet on the sunny side

of the street!" –Dorothy Fields

In contrast to Alzheimer's and Parkinson's diseases, depression *can* be

cured. In fact, it is one of the most easily cured mental illnesses in old age.

With the use of appropriate medications, such as selective serotonin reuptake inhibitors (SSRIs) and tricyclic antidepressants (TCAs), symptoms of depression can be reversed in over 70% of depressed patients. When medications fail, electroconvulsive therapy (ECT) often produces dramatic improvement (at a potential cost of memory impairment). Psychotherapy can also effectively treat depression, especially among those with fewer biological signs such as sleep problems. In fact, a combination of psychotherapy and antidepressant medications appears to be more effective that either alone.

Are older people more likely to be mentally ill?

Psychiatrist to patient: I think you are insane.

Patient: Oh yeah? I want a second opinion.

Psychiatrist: OK. You're ugly too! -Anonymous

It is true that the prevalence of the dementing illnesses increases with age, but this is more that counteracted by the decreases in depression, schizophrenia, drug addiction, and some other mental disorders. As a result, when all mental illnesses are considered together, older people are actually *less* likely to be mentally ill! This is one of the advantages of growing older – you are less likely to become mentally ill.

Why do we get slower in old age?

'Slow and steady' is the wisdom of age. -Anonymous

The reaction time of most old people tends to be slower than that of younger people, regardless of the kind of reaction that is measured. Simple reaction time (the time between a signal and a motor response) is determined by the condition of the sense organ, the speed of the sensory pathways to the central nervous system, the speed of the motor pathways, and the condition of the muscles.

However, this increase in reaction time is usually only about 13 percent at age 65, which is a small fraction of a second and does not prevent adequate performance in most ordinary activities (such as driving). Furthermore, older people who have long practiced a given activity (such as typing) can maintain their speed most of their lives. Apparently, their years of practice can compensate for slowing in reaction times.

Of course impairment or disabilities may also slow people down at any age.

Can you "teach an old dog new tricks?"

Old age and trickery can beat youth and speed any time. -Anonymous

I'm not sure about old dogs, but old people definitely can learn new tricks. They often have to learn "new tricks" in order to adapt and survive. In fact, learning new games, new hobbies, new computer skills, new studies, traveling and learning about new places, are some of the most popular activities of retired people. They may take somewhat longer to learn a new skill, but most of these differences are caused by factors other than age (such as illness, motivation, etc.).

Do older drivers have more accidents?

Famous last words: "Step on it man; we're only doing 80!"-Anonymous

One might think that because of slower reaction time, impairments to vision and hearing, older drivers would have many more automobile accidents. Actually, the reverse is true: drivers over age 65 have lower accidents rates than those under 65! Older drivers learn to compensate for slower reaction and sensory impairments by driving more carefully, driving within speed limits (something young males often fail to do), not driving after drinking, not driving at night, not driving under hazardous conditions, etc. The age/gender group with the highest accident rates is males under 25.

Do old people have more accidents at home or on the job?

Famous last words: "I'll just climb up on these boxes to…" -Anonymous

Despite the common fears of falls and broken bones, the surprising answer to this question is "No." Old people have *less* accidents at home and on the job – apparently because they have learned to be more careful and avoid dangerous situations and occupations. So actually old age is a safer age: on the highway, at home, and on the job!

Are old people wiser?

Wisdom is not wisdom when it is derived from books alone. –Horace
There is no fool like an old fool. -Anonymous

Old people are wiser, according to the common stereotype. However, we do not actually know whether old people are generally wiser than younger people, because wisdom is such a complex concept (combining intelligence, experience, knowledge, and virtue) that the few attempts to measure it have not been applied to representative samples of different age groups. However, it is generally agreed that life experience is a prerequisite to the development of true wisdom. Therefore, since older people have had more experience, they are more likely to be truly wise.

Do old people become more religious?

Little girl: Why does grandma read the bible so much?

Little boy: I guess she is studying for exams. -Anonymous

It is true that older people tend to be more religious than younger people. They do read the scriptures, pray, and attend religious services more than younger people. But this is not because they *become* more religious – they have always been more religious. They were brought up in a more religious era when everybody was more religious than they are these days. So grandma is not "studying for exams." She has been studying the bible all her life.

Do old people volunteer more?

The hands that help are holier than the lips that pray. –Ingersoll

The value of volunteer work in the U.S. is estimated to be $272 billion, and older Americans provide a substantial share of that work. One study found that a majority of seniors said they were volunteers for formal or charitable organizations. However, two-thirds of them were just engaged in church activities such as singing in the choir or ushering. This is not usually considered to be volunteer *work*.

One might assume that because retirees have more free time, they would volunteer more. On the other hand, one might assume that because of poorer health and mobility limitations, they would volunteer less. In fact, there appears to be little change in the rate of volunteering as people grow older. Most older volunteers are middle-class and in good health, who are just continuing a life-style they acquired earlier in life.

Are older people happier people?

The greatest happiness of the greatest number is the foundation of morals and legislation. –Jeremy Bentham

We all want to be happy and we're all going to die. –William Boyd

Some people assume that most old people are unhappy because of approaching death, declining health, income, and status. Others assume that older people are happier because they usually do not have to work for a living nor take care of kids, they have more leisure time for travel or hobbies or whatever they want to do, they have national health insurance (Medicare) and a guaranteed income through Social Security. In fact, national surveys show that temporary happiness, in the sense of pleasant affect, does tend to decline in old age; but that enduring happiness, in the sense of life satisfaction, tends to be maintained. Apparently, most older people manage to counteract the negative effects of declining health, income, and status by lowering their expectations and changing their goals in life. Remember: "It's not what happens to you that counts; it's how you take it."

Do older people have better relationships?

It takes two to Tango. –Popular song

Recent studies agree that older adults report more positive feelings and fewer problems in their relationships than do younger adults. Seniors typically report better marriages, more supportive friendships, less conflict with children and siblings, and closer ties with friends than do younger persons. This benefit of aging appears to be explained by several factors: seniors tend to be better at solving relationship problems, react less negatively to conflict, and have less stresses in their lives. But also other people tend to favor older partners because of respect for elders, a recognition that they will not live much longer, and stereotypes about elders which encourage forgiveness.

This also contributes to the greater happiness among elders.

Does an "empty nest" usually cause depression?

There are times when parenthood seems nothing but feeding the mouth that bites you. –Peter de Vries

We don't have an "empty nest." It's a "child-free home." –A happy parent

Many people assume that when the last child leaves home, the "empty nest" usually causes depression, especially for mothers because they lose their major role – child care. Actually the majority of parents do not have serious problems adjusting to their "empty nests". Many of the mothers enjoy the freedom of being able to return to their career or to start a new one. Both parents tend to enjoy the freedom from providing child support. In fact, we found that the parents whose children do *not* leave home (because they have not found jobs or a mate) tend to have lower life satisfaction and happiness.

Do old people need less sleep?

Sleep that knits up the raveled sleeve of care. –Shakespeare

No day is so bad that it can't be fixed with a nap. –Carrie Snow

Many older people (about one-quarter) in fact do get less sleep than when they were younger because of various sleep disorders caused by illness, drugs, disorders of the circadian rhythm, periodic leg movements during sleep (PLMS), frequent urination, lack of exercise, etc. However, the question of whether older people usually *need* less sleep is still controversial. There is a wide variety in sleep patterns among older persons.

Some sleep quite well. Many spend more time in bed awake than younger persons because of awakenings and difficulty going back to sleep. Many take naps during the day both to make up for lost sleep at night and because of the increased opportunity to nap that comes with retirement. Personally, I like to get nine hours of sleep at night plus a short nap after each meal! Apparently, I need *more* sleep than when I was younger.

CHAPTER FOUR: LONGEVITY

When are you old?

All would live long, but none would be old. –Benjamin Franklin

Don't resent growing old – many are denied that privilege –Bob Phillips

There may be as many different answers to this question as there are answerers. Bernard Baruch used to say, "To me, old age is always fifteen years older than I am."

The main problem with answering this question is that being "old" is usually equated with bad stuff such as senility, senescence, sluggishness, impotence, or at least frailty – so nobody wants to admit to such ailments, as Franklin pointed out.

The usual standard definition of entering old age in this country is age 65, when one becomes eligible for full Social Security benefits. However, this age is scheduled to gradually rise as people live longer. Also, one can receive reduced benefits as early as age 62. Furthermore, workers as young as age 40 are protected against age discrimination in employment. The United Nations and most developing countries use age 60 as their definition of old age.

The bottom line is there is no fixed chronological age at which one becomes "old". We like the definition, "You are as old as you feel."

Is Life Expectancy Increasing?

Yes, and that's both good and bad news. –Robert Butler

Life expectancy is simply that average number of years that people of a given age can expect to survive based on current mortality rates. Since mortality rates are going down because of better sanitation, health care, and healthy life styles, life expectancy is going up. In the USA, life expectancy at birth has gone up from about 49 in 1900 to 77 at present.

The good news is that this improves all our chances of living longer than our parents did (unless we mess up our lives). Even better, *healthy* life expectancy, the average number of disability free years we can expect, is also increasing (67.6 years at birth). Disability rates have been going down for over a decade now. This is the more important statistic, because most people are more interested in a healthy long life than in just surviving in a disabled or demented state.

The bad news is that this will increase the number and proportion of our population in the traditional retirement ages, which may cause various problems such as depleting our Social Security Trust Fund, increasing

Medicare costs, and need for more nursing homes, etc. (See Chapter Five for solutions to these problems.)

What is the maximum life span?

No one is so old as to think he cannot live one more year. –Cicero

Most of the claims for exceptionally long life spans have not been verified. The record holder for the maximum verified life span was Jeanne Calment in France who lived to be 122 when she died on April 5, 1997. (She credited her longevity to eating a lot of chocolate and riding her bicycle until she was 100.)

However, as health conditions improve, the maximum attained life span will probably continue to increase. Of more relevance to most of us is the fact that about 120,000 centenarians are alive in the United States today.

What is the secret of longevity?

French centenarian: "The secret of my longevity is three cloves of garlic a day."

Interviewing reporter: (sniffs) "What makes you think that is a secret?"-
Anonymous

Unfortunately, there is no secret of longevity. Despite the claims of countless commercials for so-called "anti-aging drugs", diets, and nostrums, there is no scientific evidence that any of these things can significantly increase longevity. Not garlic, not yogurt, not gerovital, not queen bee jelly, and not monkey glands.

On the other hand, all the things we know that can contribute to good health also tend to contribute to greater longevity:

* regular exercise;

* a nutritious and moderate diet; staying active physically, mentally, and socially;

* volunteer activities;

* a positive view of life;

* avoiding tobacco;

* driving safely;

* fastening your seat belt;

* good hygiene and medical care.

The bottom line is, "It's not how long you have lived, but how you have lived."

Can you inherit longevity?

The best way to live long is to choose parents who lived long. Anonymous

This worthless advice does point to the possibility that one of the factors in longevity may be your parents' longevity. Some studies have found that long-living people tend to have parents who lived long. However, in the Duke Longitudinal Studies, we found no association between our subjects' longevity (all had already survived to at least 60) and their parents' longevity. I think the main explanation for any association between parents and offspring longevity is "social inheritance" – parents who live long tend to have led healthy lives and taught their children healthy habits and provided a healthy environment for them.

Can Vitamin C increase longevity?

Lots of Vitamin C is just an expensive way to have bright yellow urine. – Anonymous physician

Linus Pauling, a Nobel Prize winner, maintained that massive doses of Vitamin C could definitely increase longevity. This theory, and similar theories about anti-oxidants such as Vitamin E and green tea, has not been supported by most of the scientific studies which have investigated these theories. Vitamins in general are necessary for good health, and in cases of vitamin deficiency, vitamin supplements may be useful, but massive doses do not seem to increase longevity, and in fact may do harm.

Can eating less increase longevity?

Doctor: Can you eat without help?

Patient: Oh yes! I just need help to stop eating! -Anonymous

Extreme restriction of calories in rats has been successful in extending their longevity by about half their normal life span. However, such starved animals develop rather nasty dispositions. Furthermore, this is not practical among humans, because the equivalent would be a diet of less than 1000 calories per day for most people. On the other hand, it is clear that avoiding obesity contributes to better health and probably greater longevity.

Can yogurt increase longevity?

The secret of longevity is eating yogurt and having lots of money. -
Anonymous

Yogurt with active cultures may improve digestion by supplying enzymes for the digestive track that help break down food so it can be better absorbed. There are even theories that eating a lot of yogurt explains the purported great longevity of Abkhasian old people. However, my investigation of these claims show them to be exaggerations of longevity that have no basis in fact. Yogurt has no more nor less nutrients than an equivalent amount of whole milk. Personally, I eat fat-and-sugar-free yogurt regularly because I like it almost as much as ice cream and I want to make sure I have plenty of those beneficial enzymes.

Are there longevity zones?

No single subject is more obscured by vanity, deceit, falsehood, and deliberate fraud than the extremes of human longevity. –Guinness Book of World Records.

In the mid-1970s there were many widely publicized reports of long-lived populations, not only in Abkhasia, but also in Hunza, Pakistan, and Vilcabamba, Ecuador. No one has investigated the claims for longevity in Hunza because the Hunzakuts have no written language and no birth records. However, investigations in Vilcabamba and Abkhazia found no evidence of increased longevity in these regions. Okinawa has the highest average life expectancy in the world: 81.2 years.

Why do women live longer than men?

Women may be the "weaker sex", but they have superior longevity.

Women's life expectancy at birth is about eight years more than men's. Even at age 65, women's life expectancy still exceeds men's – by about four years. There are two main reasons for this: genetic and life style. There are apparently sex-linked genes that somehow increase women's longevity. This is true of most species and may be a result of the greater importance of females in the reproductive process and survival of the species. But about half of the difference in longevity is accounted for by differences in life style: men die earlier because they smoke more, drink excessively, commit suicide more, fight in wars more, drive more recklessly (especially after drinking alcohol), work in more dangerous jobs, etc. So if men behaved more like women, they would live longer!

Why are there more widows than widowers?

Ageism and sexism combined produce powerful effects. –Encyclopedia of Ageism

There are about five times as many widows as widowers. One of the main reasons is that husbands die younger than wives. But there are several other more important reasons. First, women tend to marry older men who have a higher mortality rate. Second, widowers tend to remarry quicker and more often than widows, partly because there is a greater number of widows than widowers available for remarriage, and partly because our society allows widowers to marry much younger women, but frowns on widows marrying much younger men. This is a result of ageism and sexism combined.

Do Whites live longer than Blacks?

If I'd known I was gonna live this long, I would have taken better care of myself. –Yogi Berra

Yes, a White baby can expect to live about 78 years while a Black baby can expect to live only about 72 years. The higher mortality among Blacks results from higher rates of cardiovascular disease, stroke, diabetes, cirrhosis of the liver, homicide, tumors, drug dependency, AIDS, and poor health care.

However, the good news is, if Blacks can survive to age 65, then they can expect to live almost as long as Whites do (16 more years compared to 18 years for Whites). Actually, the life expectancy of Black women over 65 is the same as the average for all persons over 65. Furthermore, the proportion of the 65+ population who are Black is increasing more rapidly than that of Whites.

Is longevity increasing?

In a state of nature…continual fear, and danger of violent death; and the life of man, solitary, poor, nasty, brutish, and short. –Thomas Hobbes

Life really was brutish and short throughout most of human history. Up until about 2,000 years ago, the average age at death was about 20. Since then, average longevity (life expectancy at birth) has increased to about 50 years in 1900, and to about 75 years for men and 80 years for women at present, in most developed countries. Longevity is also increasing even among 80 and 90 year-olds. The mortality rate among these older persons is declining at about 2 percent per year in most developed countries. The remaining question is, how long can these longevity increases be sustained?

CHAPTER FIVE. AGEISM

What is Ageism?

Ageism is the third great "ism" in our society, after racism and sexism. – Encyclopedia of Ageism

Ageism, like racism and sexism, is prejudice or discrimination against people because they belong to a minority group. You may be surprised to learn that older people belong to a "minority group;" but they do, in the sense that most people consciously or unconsciously hold negative stereotypes and prejudices about aging and the aged. This prejudice often causes discrimination against older persons, such as compulsory retirement, refusal to hire or promote, and other forms of employment discrimination.

However, ageism is different from racism and sexism in two important ways: it is a new concept, so many people are unaware of it; and unlike racism and sexism, which are limited to certain groups, *everybody* will become vulnerable to it if they live long enough.

What are the most frequent forms of ageism?

Jokes are like bees: they usually have a stinger in their tail. -Anonymous

The most frequent forms of ageism reported in surveys are those involving humor: telling jokes about old people or aging; sending birthday cards making fun of old people; laughing at cartoons that make fun of old people. These forms of humor are often quite funny and seem relatively harmless; but they usually reinforce a negative stereotype about aging and therefore subtly increase prejudice and fear about aging.

More serious and damaging forms of ageism are the various forms of employment discrimination: compulsory retirement, refusal to hire or promote older people, and restricting job opportunities and training based on age. Another more subtle but damaging form is the refusal to give equal medical treatment to old people because of their age. These refusals are based on assumptions about an ailment, such as "that's just normal aging," "A person your age is not a good candidate for that treatment," or "at your age, you just have to learn to live with it."

Is ageism as bad as racism or sexism?

Older black women suffer from triple jeopardy: ageism, racism, and sexism.

-Encyclopedia of Ageism

Civil rights leaders assert that racism results in the most serious inequality, whereas feminist leaders assert that sexism is a more serious problem. Certainly sexism affects more persons than does ageism or racism, since women are over half the population.

But some gerontologists assert that ageism is becoming at least as important as racism and sexism, but is less recognized because it is a relatively recent concept. On the other hand, others assert that policy makers and the public view age discrimination as less pervasive and less insidious than race or sex discrimination. They say that the courts have been consistently unsympathetic to the view that age discrimination should be legally proscribed.

Which "ism" produces more inequality depends on which dimension is being measured. Age inequality is greater than race or sex inequality in years of education and in the number of weeks worked. However, in terms of occupation, race and sex inequality is greater than age inequality.

Is ageism declining?

A prejudice is a vagrant opinion without visible means of support. –Ambrose Bierce.

One might think that since ageism is a prejudice with no "visible means of support" in the facts about aging, it should be declining as people learn more about these facts. And it may be.

The problem is that no one has been measuring ageism long enough to find out if it is declining. I believe it probably is declining (along with racism and sexism and heterosexism) as people become more educated and more accepting of various minority groups. Also I think the coming "boomer generation" is more likely to stand up for their civil rights and more likely to demand respect regardless of their age; because they have been doing that all their lives.

Are old people more conservative?

What is conservatism? Is it not adherence to the old and tried, against the new and untried? –Abraham Lincoln

There is a wide-spread belief in "senior power" and "age conflict" which has little or no basis in fact. The facts are that there is little difference between the generations in voting behavior nor in party affiliation, and there is general agreement between the generations about our basic value system. Older people do not vote as a "block." What little "age conflict" exists tends to focus on personal tastes and styles, such as types of music, clothing, hairstyles, tattooing, body piercing, entertainment, and sports. It is true that older people tend to be slower in accepting newer, more liberal ideas, such as abortion and gay marriage; but they are gradually becoming more accepting, along with the rest of society.

ARE OLD PEOPLE SET IN THEIR WAYS?

Bad habits make muddy ruts; but good routines make firm paths. - Anonymous

As at any age, some old people are set in their ways and resist any change; while others are eager to change and adapt to change when there is an opportunity for improvement.

A major problem with trying to answer the question as to whether old people are more or less resistant to change, is that there have been few good longitudinal studies based on representative samples of older people. Our Duke Longitudinal Studies of Aging found little or no evidence that the older people in our sample were more or less resistant to change than the younger people in the study.

Also the answer would depend on which dimension is measured. On some dimensions older people change and become more heterogeneous; on others, they become more homogeneous. Warner Schaie found that measures of "attitudinal rigidity" decreases until middle age, remains stable thereafter until age 60, and then has moderate increases.

One thing is sure: most older people have had to change more than younger people simply because they have lived longer. Furthermore, any tendency to resist change may be based on their many years of experience which has allowed them to develop good routines which are beneficial for themselves and others.

The stereotype that "old people are set in their ways" is mainly another ageist assumption with no "visible means of support."

Will there be a war between the generations?

Each generation revolts against its fathers and makes friends with its grandfathers. –Lewis Mumford

One of these days there will be a terrible revolt of the old against the young.

–St. John Ervine

Some alarmist assert that the increasing numbers of elders caused by the "boomer generation" coming of age, combined with the escalating costs of medical care and social security, will result in a kind of "war between the generations" in which each generation attempts to increase their share of public and private resources at the expense of other generations. Already there have been protests about the amount of the federal budget going to "greedy geezers", and about how younger people are not receiving their fair share of support.

However, most such protests have been relatively mild and limited. There have been no significant decreases so far in the shares of public and private resources going to the older generation. On the contrary, the resources going to the older generation have been increasing along with their increasing numbers.

This is due to a combination of factors. Younger people realize that without the current public support for the older generation through Medicare and Social Security, the older members of their family would be more dependent on their children for support. Also most young people realize that they themselves will probably become members of the "older generation" and will need such support in the future.

How do old people contribute to our economy?

My father taught me to work; he did not teach me to love it. –Abraham Lincoln.

Nothing is really work unless you would rather be doing something else. –J. M. Barrie

One obvious way old people contribute to our economy is by being stable and reliable consumers. Old people tend to have more stable incomes than young people because of their Social Security and other pensions, as well as incomes from their life savings and investments. Therefore, their consumption tends to be more stable. Because of this, they tend to be buffers against extreme swings in the economy. Boom times and recessions do not affect their consumption as much as young people's.

A less obvious way old people contribute to our economy is through their paid employment and their volunteer work. About 17% of persons age 65 or over are in the labor force, and these workers make up about 4% of the total labor force. Furthermore, an even larger number make major contributions to our economy and to their families through their volunteer work. Many organizations are mainly dependent on the volunteer work of elders. Such work has the triple benefit of contributing to our economy as well as to the health and happiness of the volunteer.

Can old people understand young people?

Every generation is a secret society and has incommunicable enthusiasms, tastes, and interests which are a mystery both to its predecessors and to posterity. –Arthur Chapman

Actually, old people have an advantage in understanding the young generation, because they have "been there and done that." Old people know from experience what youth is like. Whereas the young can only imagine what old age is like because they have not yet been there. This probably explains why there seem to be more stereotypes and misconceptions about old age than there are about youth.

It is true that styles and tastes change rapidly in modern times, so that those of the older generation are rather different from those of the young. However, these styles and tastes are relatively superficial, dealing with dress, hair, music, art, leisure activities, food, etc. Public opinion polls show that the two generations are still in basic agreement about core values such as respect for individuals, fairness, honesty, "life, liberty, and the pursuit of happiness." In this respect, the old folks can readily understand and agree with young folks.

Are jokes about old people ageism?

An injury is much sooner forgotten than an insult. –Lord Chesterfield

All the research on humor about old people agree that it is mostly negative – that is to say it is insulting. A casual inspection of birthday cards being sold will confirm this generalization. Our survey of ageism found that "being told a joke about old people" was the most frequently reported type of ageism.

It is true that the insult is often subtle and disguised as "a funny joke." This causes ambivalence in many people's minds about such humor. On the one hand, many of these jokes are really clever and funny. Some of them would be funny even if old age were not involved. —And when they are told by old people about old people, it is asserted, "It is OK to laugh at ourselves," or "Humor is a way of coping with the frailties of old age."

On the other hand, since such jokes are usually dependent on some negative stereotype about old age, their repetition serves to reinforce the stereotype in people minds. Furthermore, because many people are not even aware of how subtly insulting are such jokes, the jokes may have an especially insidious effect on people's misconceptions and fears about old age. Even though the sting of the insult may be hidden behind the façade of humor, it still hurts.

Therefore negative jokes about old people are a form of ageism, just as negative jokes about blacks or women are forms of racism or sexism.

Are attempts to look younger a kind of ageism?

She got her good looks from her father – he's a plastic surgeon. –Groucho Marx.

Attempts to look younger appear to be an obsession among many older people. Billions of dollars are spent on "anti-aging" skin creams and Botox and face lifts and hair dies and wigs to try to look younger. These obsessions are clear signs that these people are morbidly afraid of old age and its tell-tale stigma, because they think old age is a dreadful thing whose appearance must be denied at all costs.

There is nothing wrong with exercise, good diets, and proper medications to maintain health. But attempts to deny aging by changing ones natural appearance is a symptom of ageism.

Is "You don't look that old" a kind of ageism?

There are three ages in life: childhood, adulthood, and "My, you are looking good." -Anonymous

Most people seem to think that telling someone they don't look as old as their real age is a harmless compliment. It is the most frequent reaction to finding out how old a person is. The problem with this "compliment" is that it really implies, "You don't look as senile or sick or decrepit as most people your age look."

Similarly, we do not usually tell younger healthy looking people, "My, you are looking good." The fact that this is a compliment to older people implies that we don't expect a person of that age to look good. As Washington Irving said, "Whenever a man's friends begin to compliment him about looking young, he may be sure that they think he is growing old."

Thus both of these compliments are symptoms of a subtle ageism which assumes old age is a negative thing to be denied.

What causes ageism?

Certain types of personality are prejudice-prone. –Simpson & Yinger.

The culture treats the old like the fag end of what was once good material. –
Max Lerner.

There are three major causes of ageism: individual, social, and cultural. As the quotation above asserts, some personality types (such as the Authoritarian Personality) are prone to be prejudiced against old people, as well as other "minority groups." Also many individuals tend to suffer from "selective perception" in which they perceive only those things that reinforce their prejudice. In this case, they recognize as old only the decrepit and senile people, while not perceiving the healthy, active elders as "old."

But probably the most important individual source of ageism is ignorance. The average person is able to get correct only about half of the true-false items on Palmore's "Facts on Aging Quiz." This means that they have about as many misconceptions about aging as correct information.

Among the social causes of ageism, there is modernization theory (which assumes that with rapid modernization, old people get left behind as obsolete); increased competition (with the increasing numbers of old people); and "self-fulfilling prophecies" (in which negative attitudes toward old people tend to result in actions which reinforce those attitudes).

Among the cultural cause of ageism, there is the phenomenon of "blaming the victim" (in which old people are blamed for the ageism against them); language (in which most of the meanings and connotations of words for "old" are negative); humor and songs (most of which reflect and reinforce negative attitudes to old people); and the media (most of which also reinforce negative images).

In summary, the sources of ageism are so varied and so insidious that most people are hardly aware of it.

What are the effects of ageism?

Ageism, like all prejudices, influences the behavior of its victims. –Robert Butler.

The main effects of ageism are positive for younger people and negative for elders. The positive effects of employment discrimination for the young include more jobs and promotions younger workers, and avoiding the embarrassment and difficulty of fairly evaluating older workers. Other positive effects for the young include avoiding society's responsibilities toward elders, avoiding the expenses of proper care, and gains in power and prestige. These gains for younger persons are, of course, balanced by the costs to elders: loss of jobs, loss of proper care, loss of power and prestige.

On the other hand, there are some positive effects of ageism for elders: retirement benefits, tax breaks, and national health insurance (Medicare). These are balanced by their costs to younger people.

The negative effects of ageism for elders include a reduction in sexual relations, loss of productivity, effective activity, and social engagement, loss of self-esteem, and deterioration of physical and mental health.

Are old people more often crime victims that young people?

Crimes of which a people are ashamed constitute its real history. –Jean Genet

Crimes committed against elderly people provoke strong reactions from politicians and the public, and the attention given to sensational cases in the news may leave the impression that elders are a major target of violent crime in the United States.

In fact, the rate of violent crime victimization is *lowest* for persons sixty-five and older. The highest rate is for teen-agers. Similarly, the rates of property crime victimization are also lower for seniors, with the exception of purse snatching and pick-pocketing (where the rate is about the same for elders as younger persons). However, there are no representative statistics on fraud and medical quackery, and there is some evidence that elders may be more vulnerable to these crimes.

There are several explanations for the low rates of violent and property crime victimization. Elders are more fearful of crime and therefore are more cautious and avoid dangerous situations and areas. They also tend to stay home more and therefore discourage burglary and theft. Also they are less likely to provoke violent crimes by aggressive behavior. Finally, the negative stereotype that elders are poor and have little worth stealing, may make them less attractive targets for property crimes.

Why are old people more afraid of crime?

What, me worry?-Mad Comics

Since it is well established that elders are less likely to become crime victims, why are they more afraid of crime than younger people? Again there are several probable explanations. Elders may believe the stereotype that they are weak and vulnerable, and therefore are more often victims of crime (contrary to the facts).

However, their fear of crime may make them more cautious and likely to avoid dangerous situations – which is one reason they are victims less often.

Are there fewer criminals among elders?

Crimes, like virtues, are their own rewards. – George Farquhar

One of the most striking differences between younger and older people is the low rate of criminal acts by elders. Those over 65 are the most law abiding of all age groups, regardless of how criminality is measured. For example, persons over 65 have about *one tenth* the arrest rate for all offenses that others have, and about *one twentieth* the arrest rate for felony offenses. Similarly, persons over 65 are incarcerated in prisons and jails at about *one tenth* the overall rate.

How can we account for this remarkable difference between age groups? First, criminals tend to die young or, if they survive, they "retire" from crime before they reach old age. This is because "crime does not pay" or because their crime pays so well they can afford to retire from it.

Second, elders may have learned from experience that crime does not pay and therefore they give it up. Also elders tend to suffer less often from the poverty that may drive younger persons to crime.

Finally, positive ageism on the part of police, attorneys, juries, and judges may reduce the rate of arrest and conviction. There is some evidence that behavior treated as criminal in younger persons may be viewed as less serious when committed by older people. Some have accused law enforcement officials of having a double standard toward older and younger persons, except for the most serious crimes such as murder.

Do doctors discriminate against old people?

Dr. to patient: The pain in your right knee must be caused by aging.

Pt.: How can that be? My left knee is just as old as my right knee, and it's OK!-Anonymous

This is an old joke among geriatricians, but it illustrates a serious problem: ageism among doctors and other health professionals. Of course none of them would admit that they discriminate against old people, but there are many reasons to suspect that some do, at least some of the time:

* Health professionals may get reimbursed less through Medicare than they do for younger patients.

* Illnesses among old people tend to be more chronic and complex and therefore more difficult to treat successfully.

* There is a widespread belief (often shared by elders themselves) that most of the illness and ailments of elders are just normal parts of aging and nothing can be done to cure or alleviate them.

* Many health professional are prejudiced against elders and prefer to treat younger patients.

* Proposals have been made that old age be used as an explicit criteria to ration health care for chronically ill older patients.

* Few health care professional receive enough training in geriatrics to properly care for many of their older patients.

So if your doctor tells you nothing can be done about it because it's just part of aging, you might consider getting "a second opinion."

Are old people often isolated and lonely?

We're all sentenced to solitary confinement inside our own skins, for life. – Tennessee Williams.

Despite the stereotype that many elders are isolated and lonely, most elders are not, in fact, socially isolated. About two-thirds live with their spouse or family. Most elders also have close relatives and friends within easy visiting distance, and contacts between them are relatively frequent. Only about four percent of elders are extremely isolated, and most of these have had lifelong histories of withdrawal. Few elders report that they "often feel lonely."

Are old people often cranky or angry?

Anger is a kind of temporary madness. – Saint Basil

One of the most common stereotypes about old people is that they are often cranky or angry. However, most elders say they are seldom irritated or angry. The Duke Longitudinal Study found that 90% of persons age 65 or older say they were never angry during the past week. Furthermore, self reports of anger tend to decrease in old age. Apparently, one of the advantages of aging is the ability to control ones temper and avoid that "temporary madness."

Is there more poverty among old people?

Poverty is not a shame, but being ashamed of it is. –Thomas Fuller

Another common stereotype about old people is that many of them live in poverty. This was in fact true before Social Security provided an income floor for most elders. Now thanks to Social Security and other programs for elders, the opposite is true – there is actually *less* poverty among person over 65, than among those under 65 (about 10% for over 65 compared to about 14% for those under 65). The higher rate for people under 65 is partly due to the high rate of poverty for children.

Do most old people have fixed incomes?

Frugality is a handsome income. –Erasmus

Yes, most old people have fixed incomes in the sense that most of it comes from Social Security, pensions, savings, and some earnings. However, they usually are better protected against recessions than others because their income is "fixed." Also their Social Security income usually increases with the cost of living. This is another advantage of old age.

Is there a senior "voting bloc"?

The ballot is stronger than the bullet. –Abraham Lincoln

There are wide spread fears that elders vote as a "bloc", and can unfairly get advantages for seniors because of their political power. An example of this is the frequent warning to politicians, "Don't touch Social Security; it is the 'third rail' of politics. Touch it and you're dead." This may be true, but it is not because elders vote as a bloc. It is because all Americans realize that it is (or will be) in their own interest to maintain an adequate floor under retirement and disability income. If it were not for Social Security, many retired or disabled person would be living in poverty and would have to be supported by relatives and/or public welfare.

Contrary to the fears of "senior power", older people do *not* vote cohesively. They are as diverse in their voting decisions as any other age group. There is no evidence that old-age policy issues critically influence older persons' votes for candidates.

Of course organizations like AARP and the National Council of Senior Citizens lobby to protect elders' interests and entitlements, but they are unable to influence elders to vote as a "bloc."

Despite Lincoln's claim that "the ballot is stronger than the bullet," elders do not use their ballots to influence elections in their favor as an age group.

Are there more older people in public office than younger?

Gerontocracy: a form of social organization in which a group of old men dominates or exercises control. –Webster's Dictionary

It is true that there are proportionately more older people in public office than younger; and this is even more true in the higher levels of officers, such as senators, judges, governors, and presidents. This association between old age and high political office if found throughout history and across types of political systems. There are probably several factors that explain this. Older people are generally considered to be wiser; years of experience in public affairs may lead to greater success in running for office; it takes time to build up a following and a reputation for trustworthy statesmanship. However, we are far from having a gerontocracy in our society, as shown by the recent election of several relatively young men to the office of U.S. President.

How can we reduce ageism?

A great many people think they are thinking when they are merely rearranging their prejudices. –William James

Ageism, like other prejudices, is difficult to overcome; but there are several things that individuals can try. First, it is important to get the facts straight. One can easily test and improve ones knowledge about the facts by taking one or more versions of the Facts on Aging Quiz (see Appendix A). Second, when you hear someone else make a prejudiced statement, you could try to correct them. Third, you could avoid reinforcing ageism by avoiding ageist jokes, birthday cards, and cartoons. Fourth, you could join organizations that are working to overcome ageism, such as the AARP. Finally, you could adopt a healthy and active life style and become a model of successful aging to counter the negative stereotypes about what growing old means.

Remember, there are many advantages to growing old. If you've forgotten them, go back and read the Preface again!

CHAPTER SIX: BENEFITS

Are old people bankrupting the government?

Will you still need me, will you still feed me, when I'm 64? –John Lennon

In 1988, the cover of *The New Republic* showed angry "greedy geezers" with garden trowels, golf clubs, and fishing rods, presumably poised to attack and exploit society. Many politicians and journalists have periodically warned that a new and awesome generational conflict will arise because of the increasing costs of Social Security, Medicare, and Medicaid. They project that up to half of our Federal budget will go to programs for the aged and would bankrupt our government. So far there is no evidence of significant generational conflict. Fortunately, the fears about increasing costs of programs for the aged have been greatly exaggerated.

The alarming projections about the "dependency ratio" (the number of persons age 65 and over divided by the number between 18 and 64) tells only half the story. The other half is that, because of declining birth rates, the decrease in numbers of dependent children (18 and under), more than offsets the increase in numbers of persons 65 and over. In fact, the *total* dependency ratio (the number 65 and over, plus the number under 18, divided by those 18-64) has been going *down* since 1970 (when it was .82), is now at .60, and is projected to be only .79 in 2040 at the peak of the Baby Boomers entrance into old age. Also it should be remembered that much of Social Security benefits actually go to younger people through its life insurance, disability insurance, and survival provisions.

Furthermore, the increasing costs of Social Security can be compensated for by a few relatively minor adjustments such as removing the cap on earnings that are taxed, reducing the Cost of Living Adjustment (COLA), and gradually increasing the age of eligibility for full retirement benefits.

Actually, a greater threat of entitlements is the ballooning cost of drugs and medical care provided by Medicare and Medicaid. This is a threat to all Americans and must be solved by reforming our health care insurance system. Ours is the only industrialized nation that does not have a national health insurance program for all ages. Many argue that a single payer system, such as in Canada, would be the best solution to the problems caused by our expensive, fragmented system.

Are old people pushing up the cost of medical care?

God heals, and the doctor takes the fee. –Benjamin Franklin

The simple answer to this question is "Yes". This is mainly because older people usually need more health care than younger people. Persons 65 and over (12% of our population) account for about one-third of all U.S. health care costs. Also Medicare expenditures have doubled in the past ten years, both because of the increasing numbers of older people and the increasing use of more expensive types of treatment.

However, the costs in the final year of life account for over a quarter of Medicare expenditures. Furthermore, it can be argued that Medicare, through its various cost containment measures (such as limiting reimbursement to hospitals and doctors) and its low overhead cost (only 2%) is actually preventing health care costs from escalating even faster.

Furthermore, the various cost containment measures in the new health care legislation promise to restrain the future rise in health care costs.

Should health care be rationed by age?

Oh, let him pass! He hates him that would upon the rack of this tough world, stretch him out longer. –Wm. Shakespeare

Because older people use such a large portion of the nation's health care, some budget cutters propose rationing health care for elderly people.

They argue that elderly people will not live much longer anyway, so health care for them is a waste.

Actually, health care is already rationed by age in various ways, for example: few seniors receive appropriate screening tests for bone density, colorectal and prostate cancer, and glaucoma; chemotherapy is underused in treatment of breast cancer in older women; patients over 75 with a heart attack is much less likely to receive blood-dissolving drugs; and surgery for Parkinson's disease is less available to older persons. In fact, the amount of health care that elderly persons actually receive is not as much as might be expected on the basis their higher rates of illness and chronic conditions

Yet, age-based rationing of health care is clearly age discrimination (ageism). If health care must be rationed, it would be fairer to base it on survival probabilities or prognosis of recovery, balanced against cost of treatment, rather than age as such. Or even a lottery would be fairer than rationing on the basis of age. Furthermore, a much better form of cost containment would be increasing investment in biomedical, behavioral, and social research.

Are organ transplants worthwhile in old age?

A donor not only contributes to the longevity of another; in a sense the donor's life is extended beyond death. –Robert Butler

The answer to the question about transplants in old age is similar to the one about health care rationing in old age; the main differences are the great costs of transplants and the shortage of suitable organs for transplantation. Whether these costs are worthwhile *at any age* should be answered by a cost/benefit analysis for a given individual based on the probabilities of success and prognosis for recovery. Similarly, if there is a waiting list, priority should not be given on the basis of age, but on the basis of other factors such as closeness of match between donor and recipient, location of donor and recipient, health of the recipient, and prognosis for recovery.

Do most old people end up living in long-stay institutions?

Life is short but the art of healing is long. -Hippocrates

One of the greatest fears of older people is that they will end up having to live in long-stay institutions. However, the facts are somewhat reassuring. Only about five percent of persons over 65 are residents of long-care facilities such as nursing homes or mental hospitals. However, another two percent are in community housing with various services provided, such as assisted living facilities. Even among those aged 85 or over, only nineteen percent are residents of long-term care facilities and another seven percent are in community housing with services. However, about forty percent of elderly persons spend some time in such institutions at some point in their lives. So some savings or insurance or other plan to finance such a stay is prudent.

Are most caregivers young people?

Long illness is the real vampirism: think of living a year or two after one is dead, by sucking the life-blood out of a frail young creature at ones bedside! –Oliver Wendell Holmes.

In this quotation, Holmes assumed that the caregiver is a *young* person. But is the typical caregiver young? The clear answer to this question is "No." In fact, about one-fourth of the caregivers of the 25 million chronically ill elders living at home are themselves elders (over age 65). Another one-third or so are between 35 and 65 years of age. So the majority of caregivers are over age 35. Also it is clear that about three-fourths of these caregivers are women and the majority of them are wives, daughters, or daughters-in-law. So your typical caregiver is a wife who is somewhat younger than her disabled husband.

However, there are another 1.5 million elders being cared for in long-stay institutions. But most of their caregivers (nurses and nurse's aids) are also middle-aged women.

Do old people get more than their share of the national income?

When I was young I used to think money was the most important thing in life; now that I am old, I know I know it is. –Oscar Wilde

There are two contradictory myths about the wealth of old people: they are very *rich* or they are very *poor*. There is, in fact, more inequality in wealth among older households (those with members 65 and over) than there is among younger households. However, the median income of older households is less than two-thirds that of all households. Of course there are fewer persons in older households, but even on a per capital basis, older person's median income is just about the same as that of all persons over age 15. It is true that the net worth of older persons is somewhat higher than that of younger persons, but that is primarily due to the higher rate of home ownership among older persons.

When do you become entitled to Social Security Retirement Benefits?

Will you still feed me; will you still need me, when I'm sixty-four? –Beatles

Despite the Beatles concern with sixty-four, sixty-five was the age at which you could become fully entitled to retirement benefits from Social Security – that was the "Normal Retirement Age" (NRA) up until 2003. However, since 2003 this age has been gradually increasing so that at present (until 2020) the NRA is 66 years. This will continue to increase until it reaches 67 years. The idea behind this increase is to partially adjust for the big increases in life expectancy since the 1930's when Social Security began (and to save money in the trust fund).

However, there are other benefits from Social Security that you could become entitled to at any age, such as survivor (widow or widower or dependent child) and disability benefits. Also you can choose to start getting retirement benefits at an earlier age, if you are willing to get reduced benefits.

When do you become entitled to Supplemental Security Income?

Supplemental Security Income (SSI) is a kind of guaranteed minimum income for all persons over 65.-Social Security Administration

Unlike Social Security Retirement benefits, all persons over age 65 and all blind or disabled persons are entitled to SSI, regardless of work history, provided their income is below certain amounts. It was designed to replace the many and varied state assistance programs for the blind, disabled, widowed, or otherwise in need of welfare assistance. It is not designed to lift you out of poverty, but should be enough to provide adequate food and shelter.

When do you become entitled to Medicare?

The desire to take medicine is perhaps the greatest feature which distinguishes man from animals. –Sir William Osler

Unlike Social Security Retirement benefits, in which the age of entitlement is increasing, most citizens are entitled to Medicare if they are over the age of 65. Part A provides hospital insurance and is free. Part B provides physician reimbursement and has a monthly fee. Part D is for pharmaceutical insurance and has a monthly fee.

Does Medicare cover most medical expenses?

When a Director of a Health Insurance Organization died and tried to get into heaven, St. Peter said he could come in, but could only stay three days. - Anonymous

Unfortunately there are many limitations on how much of your medical bills Medicare will cover. First, there are many procedures and drugs that Medicare will not cover at all. Then for those it will cover, there are various coinsurance charges, deductibles, and maximum payments. So it is estimated that Medicare actually covers only about 40% of enrollees' total medical expenses. It is best to get some kind of "medigap" insurance to cover the gaps in Medicare coverage (if you can afford it).

When do you become entitled to Medicaid?

That's another advantage of being poor – a doctor will cure you faster. -Kin Hubbard.

Unlike Medicare, Medicaid has no age limitation. Persons of all ages are eligible if they meet the criteria of poverty (medical indigence) and certain disabilities such as blindness. It is a major source of payment for long-term medical and nursing care for persons with low income and few assets.

What tax breaks can elders get?

The only sure thing in life is death and taxes. –Source unknown

Despite this saying, elders can escape (or reduce) some taxes, mostly on the state and local level. Because of concerns with age discrimination, most federal age-based tax breaks have been eliminated. However, there are

numerous tax breaks available on the state and local level, such as:

* Reduced taxes for retirement income such as Social Security benefits

and pensions.

* Family care incentives.

*Homestead exemption or "circuit breaker" program of relief from

property taxes.

* Credit or rebate for part of sales tax paid.

States and localities vary widely in terms of age and other criteria for

eligibility, but such tax breaks are usually limited to elders with lower

incomes.

When can you join AARP?

AARP used to stand for "American Association of Retired Persons." Now it

doesn't stand for anything at all.-Anonymous

The AARP still uses that acronym for its name, but because they want

to appeal to still-employed elders, they dropped the "retired" from their

name. However, you still must wait until you are 55 or older to join. –And

the majority of persons over 55 do join in order to enjoy their many benefits

ranging from advocacy for elders, to special discounts on travel and various kinds of insurance. In fact, it is the largest single membership organization for elders in the USA.

When can you get senior discounts?

Senior discounts are not a kind of age discrimination – they are just marketing devices.-Encyclopedia of Ageism

Almost anyone who looks like they are middle-aged or older can get senior discounts just by asking for them. Or if you are a member of AARP of some other such organization, you can get them. If a fixed age is required, anyone over 65 can usually get them without any problem; often age 55 will qualify you.

Senior discounts are designed to attract seniors to businesses and services at times and places they might not otherwise use. Some businesses give senior discounts on certain days (usually mid-week) to attract retired persons, because business is slow during those days. Public transportation systems may give senior discounts, especially during off-peak hours, to make up for less patronage by working people during those hours. Some fast food chains give a senior discount on the total bill while others give a discount only on drinks like coffee – again to attract more business from seniors, who typically come during off-peak hours. So don't worry about age discrimination; just enjoy this benefit of old age!

Now that your questions about aging have been answered, you can grow bolder as you grow older!

Bibliography

More information on the research behind the answers to these questions can be found in some of my other books:

Palmore, Branch, & Harris (2005). Encyclopedia of Ageism. NY: Haworth Press.

Palmore (1999). Ageism: Negative and Positive. NY: Springer Publishing Co.

Palmore (1998). The Facts on Aging Quiz, 2nd Ed. NY: Springer Publishing Co.

Palmore (ed.) (1970-1985). Normal Aging I, II, & III. Durham, NC: Duke University Press.

Palmore (1981). Social Patterns of Normal Aging. Durham, NC: Duke University Press.

www.ingramcontent.com/pod-product-compliance
Lightning Source LLC
Chambersburg PA
CBHW081841280526
45789CB00007B/2524